LET ME EAT
CAKE

CW01497066

JOHANNA MOORE

WOODBRIDGE
PUBLISHERS

Forest House, 3rd Floor 16-20
Clements Road Unit #2048
Ilford, IG1 1BA

Copyright © 2025 Johanna Moore

ISBN (Paperback): 978-1-917760-17-1

ISBN (Hardback): 978-1-917760-18-8

ISBN (eBook): 978-1-917760-19-5

All rights reserved

No part of this publication may be reproduced, stored in a retrieval system, copied in any form or by any means, electronic, mechanical, photocopying, recording or otherwise transmitted without written permission from the publisher. You must not circulate this book in any format.

Under no circumstances will any blame or legal responsibility be held against the publisher, or author, for any damages, reparation, or monetary loss due to the information contained within this book, either directly or indirectly.

For Sirkka-Liisa, who let me eat CAKE...

JOURNEY

Hei,

If you are reading this, then you may either be a Coeliac, know someone who is, or just wish to explore gluten-free baking.

This is a journey experienced through cakes.

Memories are often linked to and triggered by scents and tastes.

After being diagnosed with Coeliac Disease, I lost many of these memories as there were so many foods from my past that I could no longer eat.

I set about learning how to bake and converting my old recipes so that I could once again enjoy the tastes linked to moments, places, and the people I love.

Life is enriched by family, love, caring and sharing;
And for me, by a love of eating and sharing - cake!

It's my journey – I hope you enjoy making it part of your journey.

Welcome to a feast of flavours from Scandinavia to Yorkshire!

Johanna x

About the Author

I was born in Cambridge to a Norwegian mother and an English father, and then I was brought up in Suffolk in very much 'the Norwegian way'. Outdoors at every opportunity, connecting with nature and the wonder of the land we live in. I spent my childhood summers with my Norwegian grandparents in a small summer hut just outside Oslo, and when a teenager, we would also head to Finland to visit friends there.

Study and work took me North to Nottingham, then Manchester, then finally to Yorkshire. I married a Yorkshireman, and we now live in Ilkley just below the famous Cow and Calf rocks. As our two children grew up, we stayed connected to our Nordic roots and continued to embrace our heritage.

Being diagnosed with Coeliac Disease at 40 and learning how to bake gluten-free cakes led me to start my own business, making decorated gluten-free birthday cakes. I soon discovered that local cafés were interested in buying my Scandi-inspired cakes as not only were they gluten-free, they were just lovely cakes. I supplied a number of local cafés for about 5 years.

Now, at 60, I have developed many recipes and gained so much experience in the art of gluten-free cake baking; it felt like the right time to share what I have learnt on this very personal journey. I like to think that my original training as a production engineer has helped me to think logically and efficiently about the process of baking. Being a coeliac means that I have a deep appreciation of how difficult it can be and how it feels to exclude certain foods from one's diet.

Family and time spent with them are very important to me, and I feel blessed that we have a lot of them close by. With those further away, we seek out as many opportunities as we can to get together.

We enjoy walking on Ilkley Moor and in the Yorkshire Dales, and my simple pleasures are sitting by the fire with our two cats reading or just looking out onto the garden – often with a good cup of coffee and a delicious slice of cake!

Johanna, Summer 1968.

CONTENTS

Chocolate

Coffee

Citrus

Cinnamon and Spices

Celebrations

Christmas

INTRODUCTION

This is a journey experienced through cakes.

It's a journey of recipes and the people and places they represent to me. It's a journey enriched by family, love, care, and sharing, but above all, it's a journey enriched by a love of eating cake!

After I was diagnosed with coeliac disease and started cutting all gluten from my diet, I felt great. After about a year, I still felt better, but my diet was so BORING! I had to eat the same bread, crispbread, and biscuits. Worst of all – I had no cake.

A change of diet, for whatever reason, usually means leaving something out and not being allowed to eat certain foods, which can feel very negative.

Being half Norwegian, 'kafé og kaker' (coffee and cakes) had been a huge part of my life. The variety of cakes and biscuits made for Christmas, special occasions, or just because someone is around for coffee is astounding. I missed it. I was in mourning for it. Dry, crumbly, gluten-free custard creams just did not do it for me. I longed for chocolate cake, cakes with almonds, hazelnuts, cinnamon, and cardamom: any of my old recipes, in fact. If only I could bake them. I had tried, but they had not worked. The gluten-free flours were too thin, and because they contained no gluten, they couldn't hold the rise needed. After the initial elation of feeling so well, I now had to face what my future held, and I was not happy.

Yet there was hope. I was blessed to know a Finnish lady who was diagnosed with coeliac disease when she was 70! She was a friend of my mother's and had been a Domestic Science teacher. When she heard I was a coeliac, too, she said, 'You must come, and we will bake.' Her attitude to life and the challenges it presents was inspiring. It came at just the right time for me, as I was beginning to feel low about this whole coeliac thing.

I went to Finland, and she taught me how to bake 'the coeliac way,' as she called it. It meant, in some cases, a whole new way of baking. It meant using ingredients that I'd never heard of before. I spent five days with her baking and eating. I learnt how to bake, but I also learnt that you must make of your life what you can. Rejoice in the good and happy times. Acknowledge the sad, but don't wallow. We rejoiced at the disease that had brought us together again; we laughed at ourselves and our foibles; we ate good bread and fantastic cake. On parting, there was no need for words. We had a common bond. We understood. We would meet again.

When I returned to England, I pulled out my old recipe book and began converting, adapting, and developing new cakes.

Not everyone has a wonderful Finnish lady who can teach them one-to-one through practical demonstration and involvement. Despite the initial limitations of a coeliac diet, this book aims to impart that knowledge, enthusiasm for food, and zest for life. Focus on the fact that you will be eating the right food for your body, and if the whim takes you—eat cake!

This book is intended to give you an experience in gluten-free, wheat-free, and/or lactose-free baking. I have developed traditional old favourites and some truly decadent new cakes! You can use these recipes as they stand or adapt them to your own taste, and then, using the knowledge you have gained, convert or create your own special recipes.

Most of the items in this book can be frozen in portions, defrosted, and refreshed in a microwave just prior to eating. This is preferable because the gums used to replace the gluten need to be reactivated, which improves the texture. They can, of course, be defrosted naturally and eaten just as they are; it depends on where you are!

The advantage of freezing is that you can bulk bake when you have the time and then store a variety of foods available at any time when you need them. The bonus is that they taste as if they are just baked when refreshed.

It is possible to have great-tasting foods without wheat or gluten and without compromising flavour and texture. So many of us have to adapt our diets and our families' diets due to allergies, intolerances or preferences. It only takes a little bit of determination, time, and knowledge to embark on baking using alternatives to wheat, gluten, milk, butter, etc. It also takes a willingness to experiment. The beauty of these distinctive, delicious and sumptuous cakes is that anyone can eat and enjoy them – they are not just for coeliacs.

The road ahead…
Where will it take you?
Where will it lead?
Who will you meet?
What will you eat?

A Word About –

Equipment

If you are already a baker, you will probably have many of these items. However, if you have old cake and bread tins and have recently removed gluten from your diet, make sure they have been thoroughly cleaned, or it may be worth buying new ones.

Cake Tins and Liners

I find that an 8-inch (20 cm) round loose-bottom cake tin is the most useful size, and most of the recipes in this book are for this size. The other is a 2lb (900g) loaf tin. Buy two; if you are baking, you might as well make two and freeze one! Ready-cut greaseproof liners, round or loaf, are recommended, but you can always cut your own from baking parchment. Remove the parchment when turning out your cakes after cooking to allow them to cool.

Bowls

Two large bowls, two medium bowls, and a selection of small ones.

Scales

I find that electronic scales are very good, as they allow you to weigh straight into your bowls and add ingredients on top of others by being able to zero in between. This is particularly useful for the variety of flours that need to be blended together.

Electric Hand Whisk

Invaluable! Most of my recipes begin by beating sugar and butter with the beater attachments, so although you can do this by hand, an electric one makes it much easier and quicker.

Kitchen Mixer

Not essential, but you may have one and prefer using it. Great for whisking egg whites and for larger bakes.

Food Processor

Very useful for grinding and grating ingredients.

Microwave

Essential for quick defrosting and refreshing. It can also be used to melt spreads, butter and chocolate and is quicker than the bowl-over-a-pan-of-hot-water method.

Other Equipment:

- Greasing brush
- Bowl scraper (in Norwegian - *slikkerpott!*)
- Round-ended palette knife
- Zester
- Hand juicer
- Grater
- Egg separator
- Metric measuring jug
- Sieve
- Small pans
- The usual sizes of spoons:
    teaspoon (tsp)
    rounded teaspoon (R tsp)
    level teaspoon (L tsp)
    dessert spoon (dsp)
    soup spoon (ssp)
    tablespoon (tbsp)
- Sharp knives
- Skewer
- Wire cooling rack

A Word About –

Ingredients

Gluten-free baking, I believe, is about taking a recipe or dish that usually has gluten in it and converting it to a gluten-free version.

Gluten replacements – **Xanthan gum** and **Psyllium.**

These are the two special ingredients that are required when baking without gluten. You may have heard about them and already be using them.

They replace the gluten to help give the flour used in gluten-free bread, cakes and pastry the elasticity required to hold the rise and reduce crumbling. It is sometimes better to blend the two types of gum as this seems to produce more 'gumminess' than just using one so you will often find that I use both these gums in my recipes. They are vegetarian; Psyllium husk powder is not as well-known but is available in health food shops or online. You need to find the **<u>powdered</u>** versions of these gums to use in your baking. Generally, you need about 1 level teaspoon in total for every 150g of flour.

Flours

There are more and more gluten-free flours becoming available. The recipes often use a blend of flours. You will have to choose ones suitable for your diet and taste. I use a mixture of what I call dark (e.g. Doves Gluten-free Brown Bread Flour) and light flours (e.g. Doves Gluten-free White Flour). I also use rice flour, maize flour (a fine maize meal, not gritty polenta) and potato flour. You can, of course, use soya and gram flour, although I find that for some of the lighter cakes, these are a bit heavy, but you may favour them or need to use them. For highly textured cakes, ground rice and polenta are ideal.

Choose your flour or mix of flours to suit the type of baking. For cakes, use a lighter blend. If baking bread, use a higher ratio of darker flours, and for coating and deep frying batters, use the thicker flours. This list of flours is given in order of 'light' to 'dark':

- Corn flour
- Potato flour
- <u>Doves Wheat-free Rice Flour</u>

(brown rice, white rice)
- <u>Doves Gluten-free Plain White Flour</u>
  (rice, potato, tapioca, maize, sarrasin)
- <u>Doves Gluten-free White Bread Flour</u>
  (rice, potato, tapioca, xanthan gum)
- Maize meal
- <u>Doves Gluten-free Brown Bread Flour</u>
  (rice, tapioca, potato, maize, sarrasin, carob, sugar beet fibre,
- xanthan gum)
- <u>Doves Wheat-free Buckwheat Flour</u>
  (buckwheat)
- Gram flour (made from chickpeas)
- Soya flour
- Chestnut Flour

Butter

If you can use butter, then use unsalted butter. When creaming the butter with sugar, you can soften it in a microwave just before use. Baking spreads work well, too and have the advantage that they can be used straight from the fridge. Spreads are also very useful for greasing the cake tins.

Lactose-free Spread

There are now many options for lactose-free spreads (e.g. PURE with sunflower). Any of these will work well in these recipes again, straight from the fridge.

Chocolate

Use an appropriate chocolate for the recipe. I have tried many different brands of chocolate in these recipes and found that some value chocolate, bought at a supermarket, works really well. So, it is up to you, your pocket, and personal taste as to what you wish to use.

Nuts

Many of my recipes contain nuts in some form, chopped or ground. They add texture, protein, roughage and, most of all, that Nordic taste. They can be replaced by darker flours or a textured ingredient such as ground rice in recipes where the nut is not one of the required flavours, e.g., in the Christmas or Carrot Cake. You can, of course, use ground rice, polenta, seeds or grated vegetables for added texture as well.

Eggs

I recommend using large eggs at room temperature for the recipes.

Spices

The recipes call for ground spices, most of which are readily available. One spice which can be hard to obtain is ground cardamom. Scandikitchen, which is based in London, sell it on their website. And I have occasionally come across it in the odd deli. Cardamom pods are easier to source, and by removing the seeds from about 10 pods and grinding them in a pestle and mortar, this should yield about 1 teaspoon of ground cardamom. And as it is freshly ground, it will provide a really good flavour.

A Word About –
Oven Temperatures

Ovens are usually gas or electric. Electric ovens measure their temperatures in either degrees Celsius (°C) or degrees Fahrenheit (°F). An electric fan oven requires about 20°C lower temperatures because the fan distributes the heat around. In all the recipes, I only quote the temperatures for an electric fan oven in °C, so here is a conversion chart if you need the temperature measurements for if your oven is different:

Fan Oven °C	Non Fan Oven °C	°F	Gas Mark
110	130	250	½
120	140	275	1
130	150	300	2
150	160/170	325	3
160	180	350	4
170	190	375	5
180	200	400	6
200	210/220	425	7
210	230	450	8
220	240	475	9

A Word About –
The Recipes

I have structured the recipes in the order that the ingredients will be used and provided guidance on the size of bowls, etc. You will get used to my methods, and I hope you will find them straightforward and easy to follow.

It is often best to prepare everything in the appropriate quantities and bowls first so that once you start baking, it flows easily. One of the key steps for most of the recipes is to blend all the dry ingredients together in a bowl. This ensures they are evenly distributed when added to the rest of the ingredients.

Most of the recipes can be made with lactose-free alternatives to the spread, such as milk and cream. Slight adjustments may be necessary to the ratios, and these are indicated.

All these recipes can be made using ordinary flours. To do this, you just replace the total amount of gluten-free flour with ordinary flour, and then, crucially, you **omit** the Xanthan and Psyllium gums.

Most of the cakes in this book can be frozen, and I would suggest cutting them into portions first so that you can defrost only what you need when you need it. Anything with a topping is best frozen open and only put into bags or a container once fully frozen. The portions can then be defrosted and refreshed in a microwave just prior to eating.

Finally, at the end of some of my recipes, I offer ideas for branching out on your own. Follow your tastes, and don't be timid about experimenting. Once you have grasped the basics, you can pick up any recipe book and adapt the recipes to be gluten-free. There should be no limit to what you can achieve.

Happy baking!

Life is like a Chocolate Cake

Life is like a chocolate cake
Sometimes sweet, sometimes bitter
Sometimes plain, sometimes iced

Sometimes best eaten alone
Sometimes glorious to share
The whole to be experienced and tasted to the full

Enjoy life like a chocolate cake
Slice after slice after slice
May it be the best you've ever tasted!

Chocolate

Let me eat
Chocolate Cake

My sister, mother and me on a boat to Norway.

So here we go on our journey.

And to start - chocolate cake. It is the most comforting of cakes. It is luscious, homely and heartwarming. It is the mother of all cakes.

Mormor's Sachertorte

A rich, dark chocolate and almond cake covered with a glossy chocolate topping and decorated with almonds.

8" round tin greased and base-lined

170°C (fan oven)

30 – 35 minutes

This recipe was given to my mother by her mother, and, in turn, my mother gave it to me. 'Mormor' literally means 'mother's mother.' This cake reminds me of my childhood summers in Norway when my Mormor baked, and my Morfar (Mother's Father) looked after us in the garden. We would all stop and eat cake in the shade of the apple trees. The scents of chocolate, roses and raspberries mingled in the summer breeze as the soft, lilting and comforting Norwegian language wafted around me. It was a time of real warmth and well-being. This cake is happiness in every mouthful.

Mormor's Sachertorte
Ingredients

Cake

170g	Dark chocolate - broken into pieces	Microwave safe bowl
4	Large eggs separated	
85g	Unsalted butter/spread	Large bowl
125g	Caster sugar	
75g	Ground almonds	
50g	Plain white gf flour	Blend together in a bowl
½ tsp	Baking powder	
½ tsp	Xanthan gum	

Topping

60g	Dark chocolate - broken into pieces	Small microwave-safe bowl
40g	Unsalted butter/spread	

Decoration

12g	Flaked almonds

PREPARATION

1. Melt the chocolate for the cake in a microwave on full power for 1 minute. Stir, then microwave again on full power for 30 seconds. Stir until all the chocolate has melted, and then set aside to cool slightly.

2. Whisk the egg whites until stiff and set aside.

3. Cream the butter/spread and sugar using an electric hand whisk until pale and light.

4. Add the cooled melted chocolate and mix it gently on a low speed.

5. Add the egg yolks and mix gently on a low speed.

6. Fold in the blended dry ingredients and egg whites to the chocolate mix by hand until well combined; I like using one of the electric hand mixer beaters to do this.

7. Scoop into the prepared tin with a *slikkerpott* and level.

8. Bake for 30 – 35 minutes at 170°C Fan oven, a skewer should come out clean.

9. Remove from the oven and allow to cool in the tin for about 10 minutes.

10. Turn out onto a wire cooling rack, right side up, and leave to cool completely.

11. To decorate: Melt the chocolate and butter/spread for the topping in a microwave on full power for 20 seconds, remove and stir. Then microwave again on full power for another 20 seconds, then stir until blended and silky smooth. Spread over the top of the cake and make ridges across the cake using the back of a teaspoon.

12. Sprinkle the flaked almonds around the edge of the cake. Leave to set, then serve.

---

*Freezing tip: You can slice the decorated cake after the topping has set. I usually cut my cakes into 8, and open freeze them. Once frozen, they can be stored in a plastic bag or container. You can then enjoy it defrosting one slice at a time, warming through using a microwave if desired.

Mormor and Morfar with my mother, my sister, and me.
Summer, 1967.

Grandma at 18.

GRANDMA'S CHOCOLATE CAKE

A rather special general-purpose chocolate cake for any occasion.

8" round tin greased and base-lined

160°C (fan oven)

35 - 40 minutes

From a Norwegian Mormor to a Yorkshire Grandma!

Grandma is famous for whipping up chocolate cakes when any grandchildren or great-grandchildren appear, and they get devoured just as quickly. Cakes are sent in tins to those who could not make the visit at that time and are specially commissioned for birthdays, weddings, or just to take home.

The secret ingredients – hot water and a fork for wiggling the icing!

Grandma's Chocolate Cake
Ingredients

Cake

4	Large eggs separated	
200g	Baking spread	Large bowl
200g	Caster sugar	
2 tbsp	Cold milk	
100g	Plain white gf flour	
100g	Rice flour	Blend together in a bowl
40g	Hot chocolate powder	
1 R tsp*	Baking powder	
1 L tsp*	Xanthan gum	
2 tbsp	Hot water	

Filling and Topping

175g	Icing sugar
65g	Baking spread
2 dsp	Cocoa powder
2 dsp	Hot water

Measuring tip:
R tsp - means a Rounded teaspoon and
L tsp - means a Level teaspoon!

PREPARATIONS

1. Start by whisking the egg whites stiff and set aside.

2. Cream together the spread and the sugar using an electric hand whisk until they are pale and light.

3. Fold in the whisked egg whites using one of the beaters from the electric hand whisk, and then stir in the egg yolks and the milk.

4. Fold in the blended dry ingredients, then lastly, add the hot water.

5. Scoop the mixture into the prepared tin and shake to level.

6. Bake for 35 – 40 minutes at 160°C (fan oven) until risen and a skewer comes out clean.

7. Allow to cool in the tin for about 10 minutes before turning out onto a cooling rack. Allow to cool completely.

8. Make the filling and topping by beating all the ingredients together until blended and smooth.

9. Once the cake is cool, cut it in half horizontally. Spread half the filling/topping mixture over the bottom half of the cake. Put on the top half of the cake, spread the remaining filling/topping mixture all over the top, and finish decorating the cake by creating a wiggly pattern with a fork!

10. Cut and serve.

Freezing tip: cut into portions and open freeze. Once frozen it can be transferred to a bag or container and stored in the freezer

CHOCOLATE CAKE – BASIC OR EGG-FREE

A soft and sticky chocolate cake.

8" round tin greased and base-lined

175°C (fan oven)

25 – 30 minutes

Well, this was a challenge. My sister-in-law had been advised to remove many foods from her diet. She struggled to find anything cake-like she could eat. We spent a day baking eggs, lactose, gluten and wheat-free! This just shows that one can always make something. This cake has a brownie feel to it. It is actually very yummy and certainly fills a cake requirement. She was very kind and said the day spent baking was more supportive than any of her doctor's or nutritionist's appointments had been. Of course, it was – we ended up eating cake!

Chocolate Cake – Basic or Egg-free
Ingredients

150g	Butter/spread	
150g	Caster sugar	Large bowl
1 tsp	Vanilla sugar	

3	Large eggs	
OR		
4 tsp	'No Egg' powder	Blended together
8 tbsp	Water	

60g	Plain white gf flour	
55g	Rice flour	
35g	Cocoa powder	Blend together in a bowl
1 R tsp*	Baking powder	
1 L tsp*	Xanthan gum	

*Measuring tip:
R tsp - means a Rounded teaspoon and
L tsp - means a Level teaspoon!

PREPARATIONS

1. Cream together the sugars and butter/spread using an electric hand whisk.

2. Beat in the eggs one at a time **OR** fold in the blended 'No Egg' mixture using one of the whisk beaters.

3. Fold in the blended flour mixture by hand using one of the whisk beaters.

4. Scoop the cake mixture into the prepared 8" tin and level.

5. Bake for 25 - 30 minutes at 175°C (fan oven).

6. Remove from the oven and allow to cool in the tin for 10 minutes, then turn out onto a cooling rack and allow to cool completely.

7. Serve just as it is or with cream or ice cream (lactose-free if required).

*Decoration tip:
Add a selection of nuts
to the top of the cake
eg desiccated coconut and cashews.

Chocolate, Date and Almond Brownies

A dark chocolate brownie with a soft date and almond centre with a crisp top.

My son and his friends never seem to get tired of eating these. They just melt in your mouth. For us GF people, brownies are often the most available item in cafés. They are quite easy to make and adapt to your own liking.

Make either size and bake at 175°C (fan oven) for 30 minutes.

8" square tin greased   OR   Large tray 13" x 11" greased
and lined (makes 9)   and lined (makes 16)

Chocolate, Date and Almond Brownies
Ingredients

8" square tin

115g	Butter/spread	Small saucepan
30g	Cocoa powder	
50g	Plain white gf flour	
25g	Rice flour	
¼ tsp	Baking powder	Blend together in a bowl
¼ tsp	Xanthan gum	
50g	Ground almonds	
50g	Chopped stoned dates	
225g	Caster sugar	
2 tsp	Vanilla sugar/essence	Large bowl
2	Large eggs	

13" x 11" large tray

230g	Butter/spread	Small saucepan
65g	Cocoa powder	
100g	Plain white gf flour	
50g	Rice flour	
½ tsp	Baking powder	Blend together in a bowl
½ tsp	Xanthan gum	
100g	Ground almonds	
100g	Chopped stoned dates	
425g	Caster sugar	
4 tsp	Vanilla sugar/essence	Large bowl
4	Large eggs	

Preparations

1. Gently melt the butter/spread and cocoa powder in a saucepan on low heat, stirring occasionally until all melted and blended. Remove from the heat and set aside to cool.

2. Chop up the dates. I like to use kitchen scissors to do this and mix them in with the other blended dry ingredients.

3. Beat the eggs and sugars using an electric hand whisk on a high setting until pale and thick. This should take about 5 minutes.

4. Add in the cooled cocoa mixture and whisk gently on a low setting until the mixture is all the same colour.

5. Finally, fold in the blended flour, almonds and dates by hand using one of the beaters from the electric hand whisk until all the ingredients are incorporated.

6. Scoop into the greased and lined tin and level the mixture.

7. Bake at 175°C fan oven for about 30 minutes. The top should be crisp.

8. Leave to cool in the tin before cutting. Serve or freeze.

*Feel free to add your own twist to these,
add a flour instead of the nuts. Or add
chopped nuts, chocolate drops etc.*

Our car being put on to the boat in Bergen, Norway 1971.

Chocolate and Pecan Brownies

A very dark chocolate brownie with a nutty, fudgy centre and a crisp top.

8" <u>square</u> tin greased and base lined
(makes 9 large slices)

175°C fan oven

40 minutes

My son knows that although I love my Chocolate, Date and Almond brownie recipe, variety is the spice of life. So, bless him, when learning to cook at school, he wanted me to help him adapt the recipe so I could eat them.

I must say they are even more chocolaty and even more gooey than mine. Beware of the sugar rush, as these are VERY rich.

Chocolate and Pecan Brownies
Ingredients

Brownie

200g	Unsalted butter/spread	
225g	Dark chocolate -broken into pieces*	Microwave safe bowl
3	Large eggs	
150g	Caster sugar	Large bowl
100g	Soft dark sugar	
1 tsp	Vanilla sugar or essence	
100g	Plain white gf flour	
50g	Rice flour	Blend together in a bowl
½ tsp	Xanthan gum	
50g	Pecan nuts, chopped	

*Chocolate tip: break up into pieces
whilst still in the sealed plastic packet
(don't do this if the chocolate is in foil as
you may get bits of foil in the microwave).*

Preparations

1. Place the butter/spread and chocolate pieces in a microwave-safe bowl and microwave for 30 seconds - stir, then a further 30 seconds - stir, then a further 30 seconds – give it a really good stir and then a final 30 seconds – stir until all the chocolate has melted and blended with the butter/spread.

2. In a separate bowl, beat the eggs and sugars together using an electric hand whisk on high speed for 2-3 minutes.

3. Scoop all the butter/chocolate mixture into the egg mixture using a small scraper, then beat together at a slow speed; stop once all incorporated.

4. Add the flours and chopped nuts. Beat on a slow speed until smooth.

5. Pour the mixture into the tin, scoop everything from the bowl using a scraper and allow the mixture to level itself.

6. Bake for 40 minutes at 175°C (fan oven) until the top is firm to the touch – the centre will be nice and gooey! If you prefer your brownies firmer in the middle – cook until a skewer comes out clean.

7. Leave to cool completely in the tin.

8. Remove and cut into 9 squares. They can be stored in a tin for 3-4 days or frozen.

Coffee

Norwegian Coffee Cake

A light sponge cake drenched in coffee and liqueur, topped with whipped cream and dusted with cocoa powder.

8" round tin greased and base-lined.

175°C (fan oven)

30-35 minutes

This is such an old recipe, but it is one of the first I adapted to be gluten-free, as it is an all-time favourite of mine. I love it as it combines all the elements of an indulgent moment – chocolate, coffee, alcohol and cream! It takes me to log cabin cafés with views of snow-topped mountains, blue sky and sun on my face.

Norwegian Coffee Cake
Ingredients

Cake

150g	Unsalted butter/spread	Large bowl
150g	Caster sugar	
3	Large eggs	
50g	Brown gf flour	
50g	Plain white gf flour	
50g	Rice flour	Blend together in a bowl
1 tsp	Baking powder	
1 level tsp	Xanthan gum	

Strong black coffee – 5 tsp instant coffee (decaf works, too) made with 250ml hot water and 1 tsp brown sugar.

1 tbsp Brandy or coffee liqueur, e.g. Kahlua (optional).

Topping and decoration

100ml	Double or whipping cream
1 – 2 tsp	Cocoa powder

PREPARATIONS

1. Cream the unsalted butter/spread and sugar using an electric hand whisk.

2. Add and beat in the eggs one at a time.

3. Fold in the flour mixture by hand using one of the whisk beaters and then scoop into the 8" greased and lined tin.

4. Bake at 175°C fan oven for 30 – 35 minutes.

5. Leave to cool in the tin for 10 minutes.

6. Turn out onto a cooling rack, right side up, and leave until completely cool. (The sponge can be frozen at this stage)

7. While the cake is cooling, make the coffee and add the liqueur. Set aside until the cake is completely cool.

8. Place the sponge on a serving plate or stand and slowly drizzle the coffee mixture over the cake using a spoon. Ensure that all of the cake is covered and allow it to soak in.

9. Whip the cream till it holds soft peaks and spread it over the top of the cake with a palette knife or the back of a spoon. Using a sieve, dust with the cocoa powder and serve.

Coffee, Cinnamon and Chocolate Cake

A sumptuous coffee cake enriched with dark chocolate and cinnamon.

8" round tin greased and base-lined.

175°C (fan oven)

35 minutes

I will admit to having a tendency to bake cakes and give them to people for various reasons - their birthday, if they are recovering from an illness, because I've been invited for coffee, or just because it's Wednesday! This is always a go-to for any of these occasions – the topping adds that extra treat.

Coffee, Cinnamon and Chocolate Cake
Ingredients

Cake

100g	Unsalted butter/spread	Microwave-safe bowl
100g	Dark Chocolate	
1 tbsp	Instant coffee granules (Decaf if desired)	
4	Large eggs	Large bowl
200g	Caster sugar	
50g	Plain white gf flour	
50g	Rice flour	
2 tsp	Ground cinnamon	Blend together in a bowl
½ tsp	Baking powder	
½ tsp	Xanthan gum	
½ tsp	Psyllium	

Topping (optional)

60g	Dark chocolate
40g	Butter/spread

Decoration (optional)

Coffee beans or chocolate coffee beans.

PREPARATIONS

1. Break the chocolate into pieces and put it into a microwave-safe bowl with the butter/spread, then microwave on full power (800W) for 40s.

2. Stir in the instant coffee granules, and then microwave on full power for a further 20s. Stir until the mixture is evenly blended. Set aside.

3. Beat the eggs and sugar in a large bowl using an electric hand whisk until pale and thick; this should take 5 to 10 minutes.

4. Add the chocolate and coffee mixture and beat in gently.

5. Fold in the blended dry ingredients by hand, using one of the beaters from the electric hand whisk, until all the ingredients have been incorporated.

6. Scoop into the prepared cake tin and level.

7. Bake for 35 minutes at 175°C (fan oven).

8. Allow to cool in the tin for about 10 minutes, then turn out onto a wire cooling rack, right side up, and allow to cool completely.

9. To make the topping, put the butter/spread and the chocolate, broken into pieces, in a microwave-safe bowl and microwave on full power (800w) for 20 seconds, then stir. Microwave on full power for a further 20 seconds. Stir until all the chocolate and butter/spread have melted and the mixture is smooth, shiny and evenly blended.

10. Pour the topping over the cooled cake, spreading to the edges with the back of a teaspoon. Decorate by making large ridges backwards and forwards across the cake again using the back of a teaspoon.

11. Finally, decorate around the edge of the cake with coffee beans.

Spice switch – this cake also works really well with cardamom. You probably only need to use 1 tsp of ground cardamom instead of two tablespoons of cinnamon; it depends on how much you like cardamom!

Dad on the Hardangevidda, Norway.

COFFEE AND PECAN CAKE

A brown rice flour sponge cake with chopped pecans, topped with coffee butter icing.

8" Round tin greased and base-lined.

175°C (fan oven)

25 -30 minutes.

My Dad had a sweet tooth. He had his own tin, which was always filled with biscuits or cakes. A particular favourite was a coffee and walnut slice he used to buy. I developed my own recipe, especially for him. As an alternative, I use pecans instead of walnuts. It gives a slightly sweeter cake – as if Dad needed that!

Coffee and Pecan Cake
Ingredients

Cake

150g	Unsalted butter/spread	Large bowl
150g	Caster sugar	
3	Large eggs	
50g	Brown gf flour	
50g	Plain white gf flour	
25g	Rice flour	Blend together
25g	Maize flour	in a bowl
1 tsp	Baking powder	
1 level tsp	Xanthan gum	
½ tsp	Psyllium	
25g	Pecans, chopped	

Topping

100g	Icing sugar	
30g	Unsalted butter/spread	
1 tsp	Instant coffee	Make up the coffee
2 tsp	Boiled water	

Decoration

8	Pecan halves

Preparations

1. Cream together the butter/spread and sugar using an electric hand whisk until pale and light.

2. Beat the eggs one at a time, adding a teaspoon of the flour mix with each egg to avoid curdling.

3. Fold in the blended flours and chopped pecans to the egg mixture by hand using one of the whisk beaters.

4. Scoop into the prepared cake tin and level.

5. Bake at 175°C (fan oven) for 25-30 minutes, and the skewer should come out clean.

6. Leave to cool in the tin for 10 minutes.

7. Turn out onto a cooling rack and leave to cool completely.

8. Make the topping by beating the softened butter/spread, icing sugar and coffee together using an electric hand whisk until smooth and creamy.

9. Spread the coffee icing over the top of the cake and make ridges backwards and forwards using a blunt knife.

10. Cut into 8 pieces and decorate by placing a pecan half on each slice.

BANANA, DATE AND WALNUT CAKE

A traditional banana cake enriched with dates and walnuts topped with coffee butter icing.

8" round tin or loaf tin greased and base-lined

175°C (fan oven)

30 minutes

This was a very early conversion to gluten-free and has seen many iterations - the page in my cookery folder has many handwritten scribbles on it. This is the current version – feel free to tweak it to your own personal taste!

BANANA, DATE AND WALNUT CAKE
INGREDIENTS

Cake

75g	Unsalted butter/spread	
100g	Caster sugar	
3	Large eggs	
75g	Plain white gf flour	
50g	Brown gf flour	Blend together
50g	Rice flour	in a bowl
1 R tsp	Baking powder	
1 L tsp	Xanthan gum	
30g	Stoned dates	Roughly chopped
20g	Walnuts	Roughly chopped
2	Ripe bananas (about 200g)	Mashed with a dash of lemon juice*

Topping

100g	Icing sugar	
30g	Unsalted butter/spread	
1 tsp	Instant coffee	Make up the coffee
2 tsp	Boiled water	

Decoration (Optional)

8	Walnut halves

Preparations

1. Cream together the butter and sugar, using an electric hand whisk, until pale and light.

2. Add the eggs one at a time and beat in.

3. Fold in the blended dry ingredients, walnuts, dates and bananas with one of the beaters from the hand whisk and mix well until all the ingredients are incorporated.

4. Scoop into the prepared tin.

5. Bake at 175°C fan oven for 30 minutes.

6. Leave to cool in the tin for 10 minutes.

7. Turn out onto a cooling rack and leave to cool completely.

8. Make the topping by beating together the softened butter/spread, icing sugar and coffee.

9. Spread the coffee icing over the top of the cake and make ridges using a blunt knife. Cut the round cake into 8 slices and top it with a walnut half to each slice. It can be open-frozen at this stage. Once frozen, it can be stored in a plastic bag or container.

This cake can be baked in a loaf tin if you prefer.
It also tastes just as good when eaten plain without the topping.

Lemon juice tip: Use bottled lemon juice from the fridge for when you only need a dash.

Coffee and Cardamom Cake

A rich sponge cake containing ground almonds, flavoured with the Scandinavian combination of coffee and cardamom, topped with flaked almonds.

8" round tin, greased and base lined

175°C (fan oven)
10 minutes

plus

165°C (fan oven)
20 minutes

My friend in Finland would always welcome me warmly on my visits, and we would sit and drink coffee and eat cardamom cake before heading out to the food markets in Turku.

Coffee and Cardamom Cake
Ingredients

Cake

4	Large eggs separated	
40g	Caster sugar	Whisking with the whites
100g	Caster sugar	Whisking with the yolks
60g	Unsalted butter/spread	Melted and cooled
90g	Ground almonds	
50g	Plain white gf flour	
40g	Rice flour	Blend together
1 tsp	Baking powder	in a bowl
½ tsp	Xanthan gum	
1 R tsp	Ground cardamom	
10g	Ground filter coffee	
1 tbsp	Masala wine or sherry*	

Decoration

15g	Flaked almonds

Alcohol substitute tip:
Use a tbsp of milk or cooled boiled water
instead of the masala wine or sherry.

Preparations

1. Whisk the egg whites stiff, then add the 40g sugar and continue to whisk until blended, shiny and smooth, set aside.

2. Melt the fat in a small bowl in a microwave at full power for about 30s and set aside to cool slightly.

3. Whisk the egg yolks and the 100g caster sugar in a large bowl using an electric hand whisk until pale and thick.

4. Fold in the alcohol, melt fat and blend dry ingredients carefully by hand, using one of the hand whisk beaters.

5. Fold in the whisked egg white mixture into the cake mixture until everything is incorporated then scoop the mixture into the prepared tin and level.

6. Sprinkle evenly with the flaked almonds and bake at 175°C for 10 minutes, then lower the temperature to 165°C and bake for a further 20 minutes until the cake is evenly browned on top.

7. Remove from the oven and allow to cool in the tin for 10 minutes before turning out, right side up, to serve.

8. Or turn it out onto a wire cooling rack, right side up, to cool completely before cutting and freezing.

Citrus

ORANGE TORTE

A really moist and textured torte made with almonds and richly flavoured with fresh orange and orange liqueur.

8" round cake tin, greased and base-lined

175°C (fan oven) reducing to 150°C (fan oven)

30 minutes

Over the years, a group of friends have met on a Friday morning for a walk on heather-clad Ilkley Moor in Yorkshire. But in good Norwegian tradition, we then take turns to host coffee and cake after this bracing experience. We talk about life, our trials, our joys and our children. We drink good coffee and eat equally good cake. One of the ladies is known for her orange cake – which is always gluten-free out of kindness to me. You will find along the way some people really understand how hard it is, on social occasions, to feel included when everyone else is eating lovely things you can't have. They go the extra mile and make that extra effort for you. I truly appreciate her for baking such a yummy cake.

Orange Torte
Ingredients

Cake

125g	Unsalted butter/spread	
125g	Caster sugar	Large bowl
	Zest from one orange	
2	Large eggs	
1 tbsp	Orange liqueur	e.g. Cointreau
1 ssp	Fresh orange juice	
175g	Ground rice	
100g	Ground almonds	Blend together
1 rounded tsp	Baking powder	

Syrup

115g	Caster sugar
250ml	Orange juice

One orange typically yields around 100ml of juice.
After using a ssp of this in the cake, use the rest in the syrup, topping up with a carton of orange juice to make a total of 250ml.

Drizzle icing

30g	Icing sugar
2 tsp	Orange juice

Preparations

1. Heat oven to 175°C (Fan oven).

2. Cream butter/sugar/orange zest until light and fluffy using an electric hand whisk.

3. Add the eggs and beat thoroughly.

4. Lightly stir in the liqueur and the orange juice for the cake.

5. Fold in the blended dry ingredients by hand but using one of the hand whisk beaters until they are all incorporated.

6. Scoop the mixture into the prepared tin, level it, and place it in the preheated oven at 175°C (fan oven). Immediately turn the oven down to 150°C (fan oven) and bake for 30 minutes.

7. When the cake is halfway through baking, prepare the syrup. Place the sugar and orange juice in a pan and bring to the boil. Boil briskly for about 5 minutes. Set aside and allow to cool slightly.

8. Remove the golden cake from the oven and spoon the syrup evenly over the hot cake. Allow the cake to cool completely in the tin.

9. Once the cake is cool and all the syrup has been absorbed into the cake, ease out of the tin and place the right side up on a serving plate.

10. Make the drizzle icing by stirring the icing sugar and the orange juice together until all blended and runny. Decorate by zig-zagging the icing over the cake. Allow to set.

11. Serve as is or with crème fraiche or cream.

LAVENDER AND LIME

A light sponge delicately flavoured with lavender and lime,
a taste of vintage summers.

8" round tin,
greased and
base lined

Oven 170°C
(fan oven)

25 – 30
minutes

One of my pleasures in life is visiting gardens. One particular garden I
would like to visit with my younger sister is in the Cotswolds. It has a
sunken walled garden with lavender tumbling over the sides. We walk
through the idyllic sunkissed grounds, catching up with what's been going
on in our lives, and naturally, we get a coffee and a cake afterwards.

LAVENDER AND LIME
INGREDIENTS

Cake

150g	Unsalted butter/spread	
90g	Caster sugar	Large bowl
60g	Lavender sugar*	
2 tsp	Lime juice*	
3	Large eggs	
100g	Plain white gf flour	
50g	Rice flour	
1 tsp	Baking powder	Blend together
½ tsp	Xanthan gum	
½ tsp	Psyllium	

Drizzle icing

30g	Icing sugar
2 tsp	Lime juice

---

*Lavender Sugar: Blend 60g caster sugar
with a handful of culinary lavender
flowers in a food processor. Make more if
you wish and store in an old jam jar for
up to six months.

*Lime juice tip: Use bottled lime juice as
no zest is required for this cake.

Preparations

1. Cream the butter/sugars/lime juice using an electric hand whisk.

2. Add the eggs one at a time and beat in well; add a teaspoon of the flour mix with each egg to prevent the mixture from curdling.

3. Fold in the blended dry ingredients by hand but using one of the whisk beaters.

4. Scoop into the prepared tin and level the mixture.

5. Bake for 25-30 minutes at 170°C (fan oven) until golden.

6. Remove and allow to cool in the tin for about 10 minutes.

7. Turn it out onto a wire cooling rack and allow it to cool completely.

8. Make the drizzle icing by stirring the icing sugar and the lime juice together until all blended and runny. Decorate by drizzling the icing over the cake. Allow to set.

ORANGE, CHOCOLATE AND CHILLI TORTE

A dark chocolate torte flavoured with orange
and more than a hint of warming chilli.

8" round tin,
greased and
base lined

170°C (fan
oven)
30 minutes

plus

150°C (fan
oven)
30 minutes

My husband has a thing for chilli. The hotter the better. So, when
the opportunity came to combine it with two of his other favourite
flavours, this was definitely a winner!

Orange, Chocolate and Chilli Torte
Ingredients

Cake

75g	Unsalted butter/spread	
100g	Plain dark chocolate	Microwave-safe bowl
1 tsp	Cayenne pepper	

6	Large eggs	
225g	Caster sugar	Large bowl
	Zest from one orange	

150g	Ground almonds

80ml	Juice from the orange

Preparations

1. Break the chocolate into pieces and melt it with the butter/spread and cayenne pepper in a microwave on full power for 30s. Stir, then microwave again on full power for a further 30s. Stir until all is melted and blended, and set aside.

2. Whisk together the eggs, sugar, and orange zest using an electric hand whisk on high speed until it is really thick and creamy; this should take about 5 minutes.

3. Lightly fold the ground almonds and the fresh orange juice into the egg mixture.

4. Finally, add the chocolate/butter/chilli mixture and fold it using one of the beaters from the electric hand whisk until it is all blended.

5. Scoop into the prepared tin.

6. Bake at 170°C (fan oven) for 30 minutes, then reduce the oven temperature to 150°C (fan oven) and bake for a further 30 minutes. The top should be risen, crisp and a bit flaky.

7. Remove from the oven and leave to cool completely in the tin. Loosen around the edge using a blunt knife, carefully ease out and slide onto a serving plate.

Freezing tip: Even though this cake has no topping, it is tall and has a flaky topping, so it is best to cut and open freeze it before transferring it to a plastic bag or container and continuing to store it in a freezer.

My sister and me in 1967.

LEMON SPONGE

A light lemon sponge cake topped with lemon butter icing
and decorated with chocolate.

8" round tin,
greased and
base lined

Oven 170°C
(fan oven)

25 minutes

This lemon cake was one of my café cakes, so it has been around
for nearly 20 years. Lemon cake is one of my older sister's
favourites.

She often asks me to bring one when I visit, so this is for you, sis!

Lemon Sponge
Ingredients

Cake

150g	Unsalted butter/spread	
150g	Caster sugar	Large bowl
	Zest from ½ a lemon	
2 tsp	Lemon juice	
3	Large eggs	
100g	Plain white gf flour	
55g	Rice flour	Blend together in
1 tsp	Baking powder	a small bowl
1 tsp	Xanthan gum	

Topping

30g	Unsalted butter/spread
100g	Icing sugar
1 tsp	Lemon juice
1 tsp	Cooled boiled water

Decoration

Crumble a small chocolate flake or grate a couple of squares from a bar of chocolate to decorate around the edge of the cake.

Preparations

1. Cream the butter/sugar/zest using an electric hand whisk.

2. Add eggs one at a time and beat in well, adding a teaspoon of the flour mix with each egg to prevent curdling.

3. Fold in the remaining flour mix by hand but using one of the beaters from the electric hand whisk.

4. Scoop into the prepared tin and level the mixture.

5. Bake for 25 minutes at 170°C (fan oven) until golden.

6. Remove and allow to cool in the tin for about 10 minutes.

7. Turn it out onto a cooling rack and allow it to cool completely.

8. Make the butter icing topping by whisking the softened butter/spread with the icing sugar, lemon juice, and water until blended and smooth.

9. Spread the icing over the top of the cake and make ridges using a blunt knife. Decorate with chocolate around the edge.

Lemon tip: You can use the zest from the whole lemon for one cake if you wish to make it extra lemony. If you are making 2 cakes you can share the zest from 1 lemon between the two.

Freezing tip: This cake is best cut and open frozen before transferring to a plastic bag or container and continuing to store in a freezer.

LIME AND PISTACHIO SPONGE

A pistachio-rich sponge cake topped with lime butter icing and decorated with pistachios.

8" round tin, greased and base lined

175°C
(fan oven)

30 minutes

I dreamt of this recipe one night. In the dream, I was in a café looking into a large glass display cabinet full of cakes. I clearly remember ordering a slice of 'lime and pistachio'. When I woke up, I thought, why not try it out? It's quite an interesting combination that actually works.

It goes to show that inspiration can come to you at any time, and it's always worth pursuing. You never know; it might turn out to be the best thing you've ever tasted!

Lime and Pistachio Sponge
Ingredients

Cake

150g	Unsalted butter/spread	
150g	Caster sugar	Large bowl
	Zest from ½ a lime	
2 tsp	Lime juice	
3	Large eggs	
75g	Plain white gf flour	
50g	Brown gf flour	
25g	Maize flour	Blend together
1 R tsp	Baking powder	
1 L tsp	Xanthan gum	
25g	Chopped pistachio nuts	

Topping

25g	Unsalted butter/spread
100g	Icing sugar
1 tsp	Lime juice
1 tsp	Cooled boiled water

Decoration

8 whole-shelled pistachios OR roughly chopped pistachios

Preparations

1. Cream together the sugar, butter/spread lime zest, and juice using an electric hand whisk until pale and light.

2. Add the eggs one at a time and beat well.

3. Fold the blended dry ingredients and chopped pistachio nuts into the egg mixture by hand using one of the beaters from the electric hand whisk.

4. Scoop into the prepared tin and level the mixture.

5. Bake for 30 minutes at 175°C fan oven until golden on top.

6. Remove from oven and allow to cool in the tin for about 10 minutes, then turn out onto a cooling rack and allow to cool completely.

7. Make the butter icing topping by beating together the softened butter/spread, icing sugar, lime juice, and water.

8. Spread the icing over the top of the cake, making ridges using a blunt knife. Decorate with the whole or chopped pistachios around the edge of the cake.

Bergen Bryggen, Norway - embroidered by my daughter.

Cinnamon and Spices

CINNAMON SWIRL CAKE

A rich sponge cake swirled through and topped with chopped almonds, sugar and cinnamon.

8" round cake tin greased and base-lined

175°C (fan oven)

30 minutes

Cinnamon is one of my favourite spices. It is so evocative of my visits to both Norway and Finland. This cake is based on the Norwegian and Finnish bread dough rolls filled with cinnamon, almond, melted butter, and sugar mix. I have incorporated this paste into a traditional sponge cake to a similar effect. It complements coffee so well and reminds me of sitting on a veranda whilst sipping my coffee, viewing a lake through the trees.

Cinnamon Swirl Cake
Ingredients

Cake

150g	Unsalted butter/spread	Large bowl
150g	Caster sugar	
3	Large eggs	
50g	Plain white gf flour	
50g	Rice flour	Blend together
50g	Brown gf flour	in a bowl
1 tsp	Baking powder	
1 tsp	Xanthan gum	

Swirl – half for the middle, half for the top

30g	Unsalted butter/spread	Blend together
30g	Ground almonds	after melting in a
10g	Castor sugar	Microwave-safe bowl
3 tsp	Ground cinnamon	for 10 seconds
(1 tsp	Ground cardamom)*	

Sprinkle – half for the middle, half for the top

12g	Chopped almonds	Mix together in a
8g	Pearl/granulated sugar	small bowl

* I sometimes like to add cardamom to the swirl mix but it is optional.

Preparations

1. Cream together the butter/spread and sugar using an electric hand whisk until pale and light.

2. Beat in the eggs one at a time.

3. Fold in the blended dry ingredients until all are incorporated.

4. Scoop half the mixture into the prepared tin and level. Then, using a teaspoon, spoon half the swirl mixture in dots on the cake mixture and use the back of the spoon to spread the dots into the mixture, creating a spiral effect.

5. Sprinkle over half the chopped almonds and sugar.

6. Spread the remaining cake mixture over and then repeat the spiral and nut mix on the top of the cake.

7. Bake for 30 minutes at 175°C (fan oven).

8. Allow to cool in the tin for about 10 minutes, then ease out of the tin and put it on a cooling rack, right side up. Serve slightly warm, or allow to cool completely, cut into slices and freeze.

Chocolate, Chilli and Cardamom Cake

A sumptuous chocolate and almond cake fragrantly flavoured with cardamom and covered with a glossy chocolate and chilli topping.

8"round cake tin, greased and base-lined

175°C (fan oven)

30 – 35 minutes

This cake combines the unusual with the trendy, topped off with a good dollop of traditional chocolate. A friend of mine had always dreamed of opening her own café. This cake had a special place in her heart and in her café. The cardamom spice in the sponge blends with the chilli in the dark chocolate topping to elevate your taste buds to new heights.

Chocolate, Chilli and Cardamom Cake
Ingredients

Cake

50g	Dark chocolate	Microwave-safe bowl
150g	Unsalted butter/spread	Large bowl
150g	Caster sugar	
3	Large eggs	
50g	Plain white gf flour	
50g	Rice flour	
50g	Ground almonds	Blend together
1 tsp	Ground cardamom	in a bowl
1 tsp	Baking powder	
½ tsp	Xanthan gum	
½ tsp	Psyllium	

Topping

60g	Dark chocolate	Microwave-safe bowl
40g	Unsalted butter/spread	
½ tsp	Cayenne pepper powder	

Decoration

8	Whole almonds

PREPARATIONS

1. Preheat the oven to 175°C (fan oven).

2. Break up the chocolate and microwave on full power (800w) for 30s. Stir and microwave again on full power for a further 30s. Stir until all the chocolate has melted and set aside.

3. Cream together the butter/spread and sugar using an electric hand whisk until pale, light, and fluffy.

4. Beat in the eggs one at a time.

5. Gently fold in the melted chocolate.

6. Fold in the blended dry ingredients until all the ingredients have been incorporated.

7. Scoop the mixture into the prepared cake tin and level.

8. Bake in the oven for 30 – 35 minutes.

9. Remove from the oven and allow to cool in the tin for 10 mins. Turn it out onto a cooling rack and allow it to cool completely.

10. For the topping: microwave the chocolate and butter/spread on full power (800w) for 20s, stir. Add the cayenne pepper and microwave on full power for a further 20s. Stir until all the chocolate and butter/spread have melted and the mixture is smooth, shiny, and evenly blended.

11. Pour the topping onto the cooled cake, spreading it to the edges with the back of a teaspoon, making ridges backwards and forwards across the cake.

12. Finally, decorate with the almonds, one for each slice. Allow to set, cut and serve.

CARROT CAKE

A succulent carrot cake enriched with ground walnuts, orange, cinnamon and nutmeg and topped with a simple butter icing.

8" round tin greased and base-lined

175°C (fan oven)

30 -35 minutes

Carrot cake has always been a favourite, and there are so many recipes for carrot cake. I like to blend the carrots with orange, cinnamon and nutmeg. I also add nuts for extra texture, for which I usually use ground walnuts, but this cake works equally well with ground almonds or desiccated coconut. The darker flours in this cake give it a wholesomeness, which just seems to do you good every time you eat it. It is the cake of choice after walks in the Yorkshire Dales, along with a large cup of good Yorkshire tea.

Carrot Cake

INGREDIENTS

Cake

150g	Caster sugar	
2	Large eggs	
130ml	Vegetable oil	Large bowl
	Zest from ½ orange	
2 tbsp	Orange juice	
110g	Brown gf flour	
45g	Plain white gf flour	
2 tsp	Baking powder	
½ tsp	Bicarb of soda	Blend together
1 tsp	Xanthan gum	in a small
½ tsp	Psyllium	bowl
1 tsp	Ground cinnamon	
½ tsp	Ground nutmeg	
¼ tsp	Salt	
160g	Grated carrots	
50g	Ground walnuts	

Topping – Butter icing (optional)

90g	Icing sugar
30g	Softened unsalted butter
2 tsp	Cooled boiled water

PREPARATIONS

1. Preheat the oven to 175°C (fan oven).

2. Weigh out all the ingredients into appropriate bowls.

3. Beat the sugar, eggs, oil, orange zest and juice using an electric hand whisk until light and frothy.

4. Add the blended dry ingredients to the egg mix and beat using the electric whisk until it thickens and pales in colour.

5. Fold in the carrots and walnuts by hand using one of the whisk beaters until all are evenly incorporated.

6. Scoop the mixture into the prepared cake tin and level.

7. Bake at 175°C (fan oven) for about 30 – 35 minutes, and the skewer should come out clean.

8. Remove from the oven and leave in the tin for 10 minutes, then turn it out onto a cooling rack to cool completely.

9. Make the topping by beating together the softened butter, icing sugar and water.

10. Spread the butter icing over the top of the cake and make thin ridges using a blunt knife to decorate. You can cut and open freeze, then bag it once frozen.

Orange tip: Because this cake only needs the zest and juice of half an orange, you could make two cakes. Or if you don't have an orange, just use juice from a carton – it will be slightly less orangey, but it still works – I won't judge you!

Nut tip: This carrot cake works just as well with either ground or chopped almonds or desiccated coconut replacing the walnuts – it depends on what you have in your cupboard or which you prefer!

CARDAMOM CAKE

A simple, fragrant cardamom sponge cake.

8" round tin greased and base-lined

175°C (fan oven)

30 minutes

One of the Friday walking friends has family living in India, and when I served this simple but very fragrant cake at one of our coffee mornings, it instantly became her favourite. It is now forever hers, especially on the 31st of October—Happy Birthday!

Ground cardamom can be tricky to source, but pods are more readily available. For ground cardamom, you only need the seeds from the cardamom pods. Extracting them is a bit fiddly, but about 8 - 10 pods worth of seeds ground in a pestle and mortar should be enough.

Cardamom Cake

Ingredients

Cake

150g	Unsalted butter/spread	Large bowl
150g	Caster sugar	
3	Large eggs	
90g	Plain white gf flour	
40g	Maize or rice flour	
25g	Brown gf flour	
2 tsp	Ground cardamom	Mix together in a bowl
1 tsp	Baking powder	
1 L tsp	Xanthan gum	
½ tsp	Psyllium	

PREPARATIONS

1. Preheat the oven to 175°C (fan oven).

2. Cream together the softened butter/spread in a large bowl using an electric hand whisk until pale and light.

3. Beat the eggs one at a time. Adding a teaspoon of the flour mix with each egg to prevent curdling.

4. Fold in the blended dry ingredients to the egg mixture by hand using one of the whisk beaters.

5. Scoop the mixture into the prepared cake tin and level.

6. Bake for 30 minutes at 175°C (fan oven).

7. Allow to cool in the tin for about 10 minutes, then turn it out onto a cooling rack and allow it to cool completely.

8. Cut into 8 pieces and freeze at this stage, or serve along with strong coffee after a brisk walk (optional!).

Undredal, Norway Autumn 2006.

GINGER CAKE

A traditional ginger sponge cake with added crystallized ginger and sultanas with a glossy dark chocolate topping decorated with pieces of crystallized ginger.

8" round tin

Or

2lb loaf tin greased and lined.

Ginger Cake is a delicious autumn cake, in tune with a misty morning and the sun breaking out later in the day. The addition of crystallized ginger and sultanas makes this cake extra succulent.

Ginger Cake

Ingredients

Cake

100g	Black treacle	
100g	Golden syrup	Weigh into
100g	Unsalted butter/spread	a saucepan
75g	Soft dark brown sugar	
3	Large eggs	Large bowl
150g	Plain white gf flour	
50g	Brown gf flour	
2 tsp	Ground ginger	
1 tsp	Mixed spice	Blend together in a bowl
1 tsp	Baking powder	
½ tsp	Bicarb of soda	
½ tsp	Xanthan gum	
½ tsp	Psyllium	
50g	Sultanas	Dusted with some of
20g	Crystallized ginger – finely chopped	the flour mix from above to separate

Topping

60g	Dark chocolate	
40g	Unsalted butter/spread	

About 15g crystallized ginger to decorate chopped into 8 chunks

PREPARATIONS

1. Preheat the oven to 175°C (fan oven).

2. Slowly melt the sugar, butter/spread, treacle and syrup in a saucepan, stirring occasionally until the mixture is all melted, smooth and blended. Set aside to cool slightly.

3. Using an electric hand whisk, whisk the eggs for a couple of minutes until light and frothy.

4. Add the cooled treacle mixture to the egg mixture and whisk together on a low speed until incorporated.

5. Add the blended dry ingredients, whisking them together slowly at first, then faster until the mixture thickens and pales a little in colour.

6. Lastly, fold in the sultanas and the finely chopped ginger.

7. Scoop into the prepared tin and allow to level.

8. Bake at 175°C (fan oven) for 30 - 35 minutes.

9. Leave to cool in the tin for about 10 minutes, then turn it out onto a cooling rack and leave it to cool completely.

10. For the topping, put the chocolate and the butter/spread in a microwave-safe bowl and microwave on full power for 20s and then stir. Microwave on full power for a further 20s, and stir until it has all melted and the mixture is smooth, shiny, and evenly blended.

11. Pour the chocolate mixture over the top of the cake, spreading it to the edges with the back of a teaspoon. Decorate by making large ridges backwards and forwards across the cake.

12. Decorate with chunks of crystallized ginger.

The Tinkers!

<u>*Old Norwegian saying:*</u>

En er som ingen,
to er som ti!

(One child is like none,
two are like ten!)

TUBBY TINKERS!

Makes 8 large rock cake-style cakes

175°C (fan oven)

15 minutes

Here is a nod to the Yorkshire 'Fat Rascals'. As our two children were growing up, we fondly referred to them as 'tinkers', so these are for them and all who have a bit of a naughty side to them!

Tubby Tinkers
INGREDIENTS

Rock cakes

150g	Plain white gf flour	
50g	Rice flour	
30g	Brown gf flour	
2 tsp	Baking powder	Blend together
1 tsp	Xanthan gum	in a large bowl
½ tsp	Psyllium	
½ tsp	Ground cinnamon	
¼ tsp	Mixed spice	
100g	Unsalted butter/spread	
25g	Sultanas	
25g	Raisins	
25g	Currants	
50g	Caster sugar	
50g	Soft light brown sugar	
1	Large egg	Beaten

Decoration

16	Currants
16	Almonds

Preparations

1. Preheat the oven to 175°C (fan oven), then blend the flour and dry ingredients together.

2. Rub in the fat until it resembles fine bread crumbs.

3. Stir in the sugars and dried fruit.

4. Add the beaten egg and bring together into a ball.

5. Knead lightly on a GF floured surface and then roll into a sausage of about 7cm diameter, flattening the ends as best you can.

6. Cut into 8 rounds and place on a lined baking tray.

7. Decorate each Tubby Tinker with 2 currants for eyes and 2 almonds for teeth.

8. Bake in the oven for about 15 minutes until golden.

9. Allow to cool for a couple of minutes on the baking tray before removing to a wire rack to cool completely.

Mamma og Pappa on their wedding day.
Oslo, 1959.

Celebrations

KRANSEKAKE

Celebrations in our family are heavily influenced by the Norwegian way of doing things. This 'Crown Cake' is made for weddings and special birthdays. It comprises cooked marzipan rings, but the mixture can also be made into biscuits of any shape or formed to spell out a name or any message you like! The tradition is to break it apart and share it with someone you love.

The basic marzipan mix makes one celebration cake or about 75 small round biscuits.
If making the biscuits, you might find that 1/3 of the batch is enough to start with.

Ingredients and Preparations

Basic marzipan mix:

500g   Icing sugar
500g   Ground almonds

3   Large egg whites lightly whisked with a fork

1. Sieve the icing sugar into a large bowl, then add the ground almonds. Mix well together with a spoon until completely blended.

2. Add the lightly whisked egg whites and stir in well using the fork. Continue mixing with the fork until you can bring the marzipan together with your hands to form a ball. This is quite sticky to start with, but it will eventually come together. Knead the marzipan lightly on a lightly GF floured surface until smooth.

For the Celebration cake:

Lightly grease the Kransekake tins and dust them with rice flour. These ring tins are available online - 6 tray tins with 3 circles per tin, giving 18 decreasing circles in total.

Roll out finger-thick sausages of the marzipan. Make the rings by cutting lengths to fit each circle of the tins, joining the ends together as you place them in the Kransekake tins.

Cook for 18 minutes at 150°C (fan oven) in the middle of the oven until lightly golden. It is best to cook them in batches, say a couple of tins at a time.

Remove from the oven and leave in the tins until almost cool. Ease each ring out of its tin, <u>turn them over</u> and let them cool completely on cooling racks.

Use about 150g of Icing sugar, and some cooled boiled water to make a drizzle icing to decorate.

Mix the icing sugar and enough water to get a thick runny paste. Using an icing bag and fine nozzle, drizzle each cake with icing in a zig-zag pattern all the way around (see picture). Allow to set.

Place the largest ring on a serving plate or cake stand, then carefully press the next size ring on top. Continue placing the next size ring until all the rings are assembled one on top of each other, forming a tower. Leave to set, then decorate with appropriate flags.

For the 75 biscuits:

Roll out a sausage of about 2 to 3 cm in diameter.
Cut into discs about 1cm long and arrange on a lined baking tray.

Or

Roll out the mixture using a rolling pin and on a surface lightly dusted with GF flour to about 1cm thick and use biscuit cutters of your choice.

Use a palette knife to lift and place the biscuits on a greased or lined baking tray and bake for 18-20 minutes at 150°C (fan oven); they should be lightly golden.

Leave it on the baking tray for about 5 minutes, then transfer it to a cooling rack to cool completely.

Once cool, the biscuits should be stored in an airtight tin.

Quantities for the biscuits:

25 biscuits:

166g   Icing sugar
166g   Ground almonds
1 Large egg white

50 biscuits

333g Icing sugar
333g Ground almonds
2 Large egg whites

17th May, 1971.

ALMOND AND HAZELNUT TORTE

A traditional Norwegian cake with a rich almond, hazelnut and sherry top layer on a cinnamon pastry base.

8" Round tin greased and base-lined

170°C (fan oven)

35 minutes

This cake is called Fyrstekake in Norway and means Prince's cake. One of its features is the lattice top, created by decorating it with strips of pastry. For this, a wiggly pastry cutter makes the strips look more authentic, but of course, they can be cut straight. This is one of the cakes often made for 17th May - Norway's National Day. Many of my 17th May celebration memories are from when I was a child. A group of expat Norwegians used to meet up, dress in their national costumes and parade around the garden waving Norwegian flags. Funny how it all seemed so normal!

Almond and Hazelnut Torte
Ingredients

Cake pastry base and lattice

100g	Plain white gf flour	
100g	Rice flour	
25g	Brown gf flour	Blend together
25g	Maize flour	in a large bowl
1 tsp	Baking powder	
1 tsp	Xanthan gum	
½ tsp	Psyllium	
100g	Unsalted butter/spread	
80g	Caster sugar	
20g	Granulated sugar	Blend together
½ tsp	Ground cinnamon	
2 tbsp	Milk or water	

Topping

200g	Icing sugar
150g	Ground almonds
50g	Chopped hazelnuts
2	Large eggs, beaten
2 ssp	Sherry

PREPARATIONS

1. Rub the fat into the blended flour mix until it resembles fine bread crumbs.

2. Stir in the sugars and cinnamon.

3. Add the milk or water and bring together into a ball to form the pastry and knead lightly.

4. Reserve 100g of this pastry for the lattice decoration.

5. Press the rest of the pastry into the prepared tin evenly.

6. Make the topping by blending the almonds, hazelnuts and icing sugar together. Add the beaten egg and sherry. Mix well and scoop over the pastry and level.

7. Roll out the 100g of pastry to about 20cm long and about 6cm wide. Cut into 6 strips about 1cm with a knife or using a crinkled pastry wheel cutter if you have one.

8. Place these strips over cake 3 in one direction and 3 in the other to create a lattice pattern.

9. Bake at 170°C (fan oven) for 35 minutes. The top should be golden and crisp.

10. Remove from the oven and allow to cool in the tin for 15 mins.

11. Gently loosen around the cake using a blunt knife, then ease out of the tin and place, right side up, on a plate and serve as is or with pouring or whipped cream.

12. If freezing, allow it to cool completely, cut into slices, bag and freeze.

Our Finnish Friend, 1968.

'I have learned what happens is best.'

TOSCAPIIRAKKA – TOSCA!

A layer of vanilla sponge topped with
flaked almonds set in a light creamy caramel.

Makes one large tray

16 generous slices

35cm x 28cm
greased and lined

175ºC fan oven

This recipe comes from my Mother's dear Finnish friend. It may look simple, but it is a cake of operatic pretensions. On tasting it, I once had someone ask me to marry him – this cake could change your life!

Tosca

Ingredients

Base

3	Large eggs	
175g	Caster sugar	Whisk together
1 ½ tsp	Vanilla sugar/essence	
¾ tsp	Psyllium	
195g (*210g)	Plain white gf flour	
45g (*70g)	Maize flour	Blend together
2 tsp	Baking powder	
1 tsp	Xanthan gum	
75ml	Milk/Soya cream	
225g (*200g)	Butter (*spread)	Melted

Almond caramel topping

75g	Butter/spread	
145g	Granulated sugar	Melt in a pan
75ml	Double cream/Soya cream	
30g	Plain white gf flour	
120g	Flaked almonds	

*If using a butter spread or a lactose-free spread, follow the measurements in brackets for the items indicated.

Preparations

1. Whisk the eggs, caster sugar and psyllium for about 15 minutes until they are really thick. This is most easily done in an electric stand mixer at high speed with a whisk attachment.

2. Change to a beater attachment, add the flour blend, melted butter/spread, and milk/soya cream alternately and lightly mix together at a low speed until all is in and blended.

3. Pour the mixture into the lined tin and spread out evenly and level.

4. Bake for about 10 minutes at 175ºC (fan oven) until lightly browned.

5. Meanwhile, gently melt the topping ingredients, except the almonds, in a pan, stirring until the sugar has dissolved and the mixture has thickened a little, then stir in the almonds.

6. Remove the base from the oven and allow to cool a little.

7. Turn the oven up to 190ºC (fan oven).

8. Spread the almond caramel mixture evenly over the base right to the edges.

9. Bake for about 10 minutes at 190ºC (fan oven) until lightly browned.

10. Remove and allow to cool completely in the tray.

11. Cut into 16 pieces, serve as is or with a dollop of whipped cream.

VICTORIA SANDWICH

A traditional Victoria sponge cake with buttercream
and raspberry jam in the middle.

8" round tin greased and
base-lined.

175°C (fan oven)

25 – 30 minutes

This is great for a birthday or just for afternoon tea. It's a basic recipe
but by no means a basic cake. The taste is enhanced by the addition
of vanilla butter icing and raspberry jam. I've made many uniquely
decorated birthday cakes over the years for my family and for others.
I felt it was important for Coeliac children to have a cake made
especially for them. One mum said, 'I needn't have bought any
presents; all he loved was the cake!'

Victoria Sandwich
Ingredients

Cake

200g	Unsalted butter/spread	Large bowl
200g	Caster sugar	
4	Large eggs	
150g	Plain white gf flour	
50g	Rice flour	Blend together
1 R tsp *	Baking powder	in a bowl
1 L tsp *	Xanthan gum	

Fillings

3 tbsp	Raspberry Jam	
30g	Unsalted butter/spread	
95g	Icing sugar	Cream together
1 tsp	Vanilla sugar or essence	
2 tsp	Cooled boiled water	

Decoration

Simply dust the top with sifted icing sugar, or you can use ready-made fondant icing and create your own design for a special birthday cake.

Measuring tip:
R tsp - means a Rounded teaspoon and
L tsp - means a Level teaspoon!

PREPARATIONS

1. Beat the butter/spread and sugars until creamy and pale using an electric hand whisk.

2. Add the eggs one at a time and beat in, adding a teaspoon of the flour blend with each egg to prevent curdling.

3. Fold in the remaining blended flour mixture using a beater from the hand whisk.

4. Scoop into the 8" greased and lined tin.

5. Bake for 25-30 minutes at 175°C (fan oven).

6. Leave it in the tin for 10 minutes to cool slightly, then turn it out onto a cooling rack and allow it to cool completely.

7. Cut the sponge in half horizontally and spread the middle with raspberry jam and then the buttercream, replace the top, then dust with icing sugar.

8. You can cut into 8 and freeze at this stage. Or it will keep in an airtight tin for 2 – 3 days.

You can also use the cake recipe mix to make buns and decorate them to your own design.

BLØTEKAKE

When the National Day of Norway comes around – 17th May – there are parades throughout the country; people wear their national costumes, wave flags, watch and listen to marching bands, eat traditional food and celebrate with family and friends.

8" round tin greased and lined

160°C Fan oven

35 – 40 minutes

Bløtekake features highly in those traditions. A light sponge cake with custard, cream and fruit. It contains all the colours of the Norwegian flag – and it is a delicious taste of early summer – a fantastic celebration cake!

BLØTEKAKE

INGREDIENTS

Sponge Cake

4	Large eggs	
140g	Caster sugar	Large bowl
1 tsp	Vanilla sugar/essence	
70g	Plain white gf flour	
70g	Rice flour	
1 tsp	Baking powder	Blend together
½ tsp	Xanthan gum	
¼ tsp	Psyllium	

Fillings & Topping

250ml	Double or whipping cream
1 tbsp	Icing sugar
100ml	Good quality ready-made custard
Some	Milk
Some	Strawberry jam
A mix of	Blueberries, raspberries and strawberries, or fruit of your choice

Preparations

1. Beat the eggs and sugars together using an electric hand beater at a high speed until they are thick and pale – this should take about 6 – 8 minutes. This will help the sponge cake to rise and be airy and light.

2. Sift the blended dry ingredients over the egg mixture and gently fold in using one of the beaters from the hand mixer – stop folding as soon as it is all mixed in.

3. Scoop into the prepared tin and bake at 160°C (fan oven) for 35 – 40 minutes. It should be lightly golden, and the skewer should come out clean.

4. Allow it to cool in the tin for 10 minutes, turn it out and allow it to cool completely on a cooling rack (the sponge cake can be frozen at this stage).

5. Prepare the cream filling by whipping the cream and the icing sugar until stiff.

6. To create the bløtekake, cut the sponge cake horizontally into 3 separate layers.

7. Place the bottom layer on your serving plate or stand and spoon over some milk (this will help to soften the cake), and follow this with a thin spreading of strawberry jam.

8. Spread half the custard on this first layer and then a thin layer of the stiff cream – it doesn't matter if these mix a bit – and put a few of your fruits in there, too.

9. Place the next sponge layer on top and repeat the milk, jam, custard, cream and fruit – making sure you have reserved enough cream to cover the top and sides of the cake.

10. Place the top sponge on and spread the remaining cream all over the cake.

11. Finally, decorate it with fruits, being as fancy as you like.

12. This is one of those cakes that tastes better for having rested a little so that the custard and cream have time to soak into the sponge. It can be prepared a day ahead and kept in the fridge. Of course, you can serve it immediately! Enjoy!

17ᵗʰ May bouquets.

Dale horse Christmas Stockings

Christmas

Mum, in her traditional Norwegian bunad,
which is worn for special occasions and at Jul (Christmas).

FINSKE PINNER

A simple melt-in-your-mouth shortbread biscuit topped with chopped almonds and pearl sugar.

Makes about 30

Chilling time 30 minutes

180°C Fan oven

15 minutes

The Norwegians go biscuit crazy at Christmas! They traditionally bake seven different types of biscuits to share with visiting family and friends. I remember early on in my childhood that my mother would make five different types – there were limitations due to lack of the appropriate equipment or ingredients, but as the years went on, this reduced to two! I have included here the two which went the distance and have remained to this day, for us as a family, the biscuits of Christmas.

FINSKE PINNER
INGREDIENTS

Biscuits

175g	Plain white gf flour	
50g	Rice flour	
50g	Potato flour	Blend together
½ tsp	Baking powder	in a large bowl
1 tsp	Xanthan gum	
½ tsp	Psyllium	
175g	Unsalted butter/spread	
80g	Caster sugar	

Decoration

1	Egg white
10g	Pearl sugar/granulated sugar
20g	Chopped almonds

You can omit the decoration and use the biscuit mix to make plain shortbread either in a tin or rounds - just make the 'sausages' at stage 4 to the required diameter. Note: you may need to bake them for longer.

PREPARATIONS

1. Rub the unsalted butter/spread into the blended flour mixture.

2. Add the sugar when the mixture resembles breadcrumbs.

3. Bring them together into a dough.

4. Roll into sausages about 3cm in diameter.

5. Place on a board and put in the fridge for at least 30 minutes.

6. Slice into rounds about 1cm thick and place on two greased or lined baking trays.

7. Lightly whisk the egg white with a fork and brush over the tops of the biscuits. Sprinkle each biscuit with the sugar and chopped almonds, pressing them in a little to secure them.

8. Bake for 15 minutes at 180°C (fan oven) until golden.

9. Leave to cool on the baking tray for about 5 minutes, then lift the biscuits with a palette knife onto a cooling rack and leave to cool completely.

10. Store in an airtight tin.

PEPPERKAKER

Snappy little ginger biscuits.

Makes about
60 biscuits

Chilling time
30 minutes

175°C Fan oven
5 -7 minutes

Two baking trays
lined with baking
parchment.

A very old family recipe for the second of the Christmas biscuits. These are best dipped in hot coffee to savour the spicy, warming flavour, which, for me, sums up the taste of Christmas.

Pepperkaker

Ingredients

Biscuits

75g	Unsalted butter/spread	
75g	Caster sugar	Weigh into a pan
75g	Golden syrup	

100g	Plain white gf flour	
100g	Rice flour	
1 tsp	Ground cinnamon	
½ tsp	Ground ginger	Blend together
½ tsp	Ground cloves	in a bowl
½ tsp	Bicarb of soda	
½ tsp	Xanthan gum	
¼ tsp	Psyllium	

10g	Flaked almonds to decorate

Pepperkaker mixture rolled into sausages and ready for the fridge.

Preparations

1. Melt the fat, syrup and sugar in a saucepan on low heat.

2. Heat slowly, stirring occasionally, until all the sugar has melted. Set aside to cool for about 10-15 minutes.

3. Blend the dry ingredients in a large bowl.

4. Add the melted mixture to the dry ingredients and stir well.

5. Bring them together into a ball and then roll them into sausages about 3cm in diameter. Put these onto a chopping board and then into the fridge for at least 30 minutes. If the mixture is still a little warm, these may not stay completely round, but this is fine – the biscuits will just end up a little oval.

6. Slice into thin rounds, about 3mm thick, and place on the prepared baking trays. Press bits of flaked almonds into the centre of some of the biscuits to decorate.

7. Bake for 5-7 minutes at 175°C (fan oven) until golden and crisp.

8. Leave to cool on the baking tray for about 5 minutes, then lift the biscuits, using a palette knife, onto a wire cooling rack and leave to cool completely.

9. Store in an airtight tin.

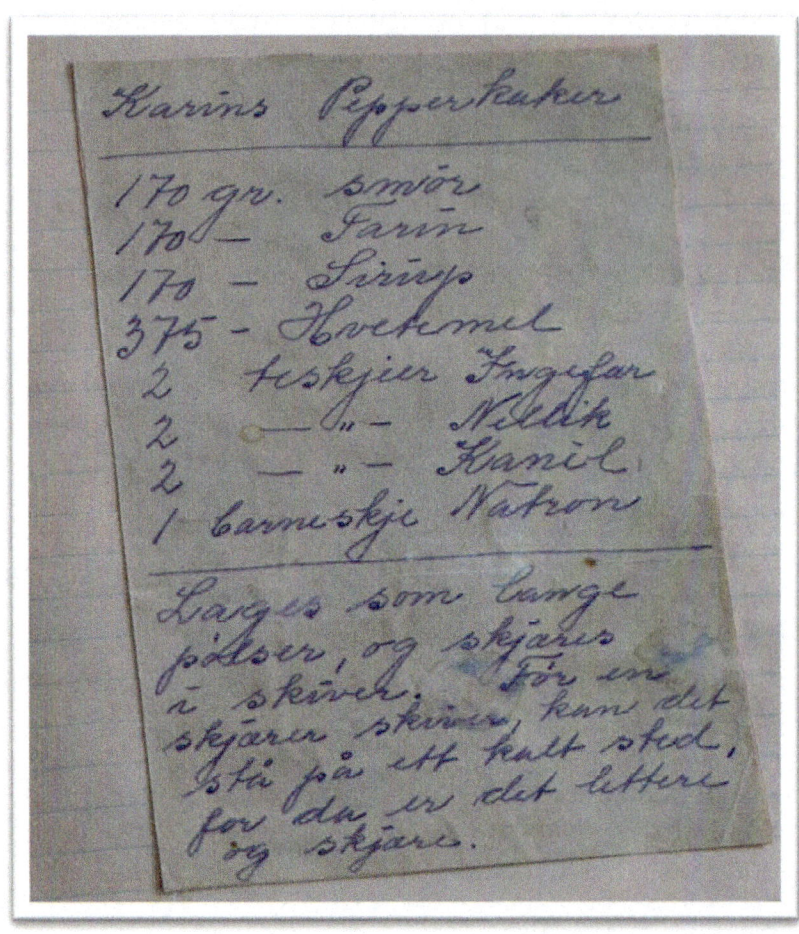

The pepperkaker recipe came from my Great Auntie Karin.

TRUFFLE TORTE

A rich chocolate pastry base topped with a dark chocolate and double cream truffle laced with brandy.

8" round tin greased and base-lined

170°C Fan oven

10 – 15 mins

Chilling time 2 hours

This has become a super alternative Christmas or New Year dessert. It is also great for any celebratory gathering as it can be prepared ahead of time. This rich, velvety chocolate torte is really decadent but quite simple to make.

TRUFFLE TORTE
INGREDIENTS

Pastry

75g	Plain white gf flour	
50g	Rice flour	
25g	Cocoa powder	Blend together
½ tsp	Baking powder	
½ tsp	Xanthan gum	
100g	Unsalted butter	
40g	Caster sugar	

Topping

250ml	Double cream
250g	Dark chocolate, broken into pieces
40g	Unsalted butter
2 tbsp	Brandy
2 tsp	Cocoa powder for decoration

Preparations

1. Rub the butter into the flour mix. Add the sugar just before the mix begins to bind together, then continue to rub in, and finally bring it together into a ball.

2. Press the pastry as evenly as you can over the base of the prepared tin and bake for about 10-15 minutes at 170°C (fan oven). The surface should have levelled. Remove from the oven and leave to cool in the tin.

3. Make the topping by putting the cream into a saucepan and bringing it slowly to just under a boil. Remove from the heat and stir in the chocolate and butter until melted. You may need to put this back on low heat to ensure all the chocolate and butter melt.

4. Finally, turn off the heat and stir in the brandy until fully blended and smooth.

5. Pour into the tin over the pastry base. Shake the tin gently to level the mixture.

6. Place in the fridge for at least 2 hours to set. You can prepare this the day before and set it overnight.

7. Just before serving, remove from the fridge for about 10 minutes. Ease the torte out of the tin but leave it on the tin base; place on a serving plate and cut into slices to serve.

8. A puree made from rhubarb flavoured with star anise goes really well with this, but you could use blackcurrant jam or just serve with cream and a dusting of cocoa powder.

Cooking our Juluften meal.

Christmas in Norway is celebrated on Christmas Eve. In our family, this is a meal of roast pork, roast potatoes, carrots, peas and boiled sour cabbage cooked with caraway seeds, called Surcal. This is all washed down with a shot or two of aquavit. Dessert is either a very rich chocolate torte or whipped cream with cloudberry jam stirred through it. And then, after all is cleared away, we get to open our presents!

God Jul!

CHRISTMAS CAKE – FRUIT CAKE

A traditional fruit cake.

The secret to this cake is the week-long soaking of the dried fruit in a combination of cold tea and alcohol. A wise old lady told me this technique. She specifically told me to use sherry! This is my offering, which does indeed include sherry but also cold tea, ginger wine and brandy. You can mix and match these but keep the overall quantity of liquid the same. Create your own mix!

I have made this fruit cake with just cold tea very successfully; just replace all the alcohol amounts with cold tea!

I try to begin my Christmas cake making at the end of October. This gives plenty of time for soaking the fruit and baking the cake so it has time to mature before Christmas.

I use sultanas, raisins and currants, as this is my preferred mix. You can adjust the combination to your own taste and include candied peel and cherries if you like; just keep the overall quantity of fruit the same.

This also goes for the flours; as long as the total is the same you can use a mix you prefer. Flour can also be substituted for the ground almonds if you do not wish to use nuts.

I hope this gives you enough flexibility and confidence to create a celebration cake that meets your own requirements.

CHRISTMAS CAKE – FRUIT CAKE
INGREDIENTS

Cake 8" Round

340g	Sultanas
280g	Raisins
100g	Currants
5 tbsp	Strong tea (cold)
3 tbsp	Sherry
3 tbsp	Ginger wine
3 tbsp	Brandy

80g	Plain white gf flour	
40g	Rice flour	
40g	Brown gf flour	
20g	Maize flour	
40g	Ground almonds	Blend together all
1½ tsp	Mixed spice	the dry ingredients
1½ tsp	Baking powder	
1½ tsp	Xanthan gum	
½ tsp	Psyllium	
½ tsp	Salt	

180g	Butter/spread
160g	Soft light brown sugar
3	Large eggs
1 ssp	Black treacle

PREPARATION

Stage 1 - Fruit Soaking

Put all the dried fruit into a large bowl and rinse thoroughly with cold water. Drain and put back into the bowl. Pour over the cold tea, sherry, ginger wine, and brandy and stir well. Cover and leave to stand at least overnight (a plastic container with a lid is ideal for this). For best results, leave it somewhere cool for up to a week. Stir daily and add more liquid if necessary. This makes for a really moist and flavoursome cake.

Stage 2 - Preparing the Tin

Double-line your tin with greaseproof paper on the base and sides and grease well. Put 2 layers of brown paper around the outside of the tin, coming 5cm higher than the tin itself and secure it with string. I use the next size-up tin as well to provide extra insulation, so I sit the prepared 8" tin inside a 9" tin.

Stage 3 - Cake Baking

1. Blend all the dry ingredients together in a bowl.

2. Put the butter/spread and sugar into a large bowl and beat until smooth and pale using an electric hand whisk on a high setting.

3. Beat the eggs one at a time adding a heaped teaspoonful of the blended dry ingredients with each egg.

4. Stir in the treacle.

5. Thoroughly fold in the rest of the blended dry ingredients using a beater from the hand whisk.

155

6. Finally, stir in all the fruit with their juices.

7. Scoop into the prepared tin and make a slight indent in the centre of the cake to allow for rising when baking.

8. Bake at 150°C (fan oven) for 1 hour and 30 minutes. Then, lower the oven to 140°C (fan oven) and bake for a further 1 hour and 30 minutes.

9. Test with a skewer to ensure that the centre is cooked – the skewer should come out clean.

10. Leave to cool completely in the tin.

11. When cold, turn it out onto its top and wrap it, first in a layer of greaseproof paper, then in a tight layer of foil. Leave somewhere cool and dark to mature.

Decoration:

Apricot jam
Marzipan
Ready to roll icing

When ready to decorate, brush the top of the cake with warmed apricot jam. Roll out the marzipan to the required thickness and size and place it on the cake. I usually only put marzipan on the top of the cake and use the cake tin bottom to help with sizing. Brush the marzipan and sides of the cake with more warmed apricot jam. Roll out the icing to the required size and place over the cake. Create your cake design however you like – simple or fancy – it's your choice!

Grandma's 90th Birthday Cake – she loves peach roses!

Sticky Toffee Pudding

A truly decadent pudding enriched with dates served with
a creamy toffee and pecan sauce.

2lb loaf tin
greased and lined

180°C fan oven

25-30 minutes

Serves 4

As well as celebrating Juluften in my Mother's Norwegian way, we also celebrated Christmas Day in my Father's English way with roast turkey and all the trimmings, followed by a rich Christmas pudding. Now, as we develop our own family traditions, we change the pudding as my husband has always preferred sticky toffee pudding. I love the way traditions evolve over the years and how they come to stand for events and people within families. Sometimes, it's good to look at why we do things the way we do, and it usually means we have incorporated love into our way of life to take account of a special moment, place or person.

STICKY TOFFEE PUDDING
INGREDIENTS

Pudding

90g	Stoned and chopped dates	
1 tsp	Vanilla sugar or essence	Small bowl
½ tsp	Instant coffee granules	
½ tsp	Bicarb of soda	
90ml	Boiling water	
40g	Unsalted butter/spread	Large bowl
80g	Caster sugar	
1	Large egg	
60g	Plain white gf flour	
30g	Brown gf flour	Blend together
1 tsp	Baking powder	in a small bowl
½ tsp	Psyllium	

Sauce *

120g	Soft dark brown sugar	
70g	Unsalted butter/spread	Heat gently in a
4 tbsp	Double cream	saucepan
20g	Chopped pecans	

160

Preparations

1. Pour the boiling water over the dates, vanilla sugar, coffee and bicarb of soda into a small bowl. Stir and leave to cool.

2. Cream the sugar and butter/spread using an electric hand whisk.

3. Add the egg and whisk until pale and fluffy.

4. Fold in the blended dry ingredients by hand using one of the hand whisk beaters.

5. Finally, fold in the date mixture; it will be quite runny.

6. Scoop into the greased and lined loaf tin and allow to level.

7. Bake for 25-30 minutes at 180°C (fan oven). A skewer should come out clean.

8. Leave to cool in the tin for 10 minutes before lifting out.

9. Gently heat the sauce ingredients in a pan, stirring occasionally until everything has melted and the sugar has dissolved. Stir in the chopped pecans.

10. Cut the pudding into 4 portions, pour over the sauce and serve immediately. Or let the pudding cool completely, then cut it and freeze it at this stage. The sauce can also be frozen. To refresh: microwave, defrost and reheat just prior to serving. Serve with additional cream or ice-cream for a truly decadent dessert!

Sauce tip:
Make double quantity in case this sauce goes down really well or use the extra on ice-cream!

MINCE PIES

Classic mince pies, makes 12.

Christmas can be an especially hard time for Coeliacs with all the tempting foods that come out for the season. Often, these are not replicated for Coeliacs, so it can be a time when it brings home most poignantly what we are missing. It is also a time of traditions both cultural and family. We want to feel we can acknowledge our past Christmases and celebrate in our own particular ways. And this is where we come full circle. The Doctor who diagnosed me was herself diagnosed with CD just before a Christmas. And it was homemade mince pies she would miss the most. May we all gain strength by knowing we are now eating the right foods for a healthy positive life.

MINCE PIES
INGREDIENTS

Pastry

100g	Plain white gf flour	
75g	Rice flour	
25g	Brown gf flour	Blend together
1 tsp	Baking powder	in a large bowl
½ tsp	Xanthan gum	
½ tsp	Psyllium	
100g	Unsalted butter/spread	
25g	Caster sugar	
6 tsp	Cold water	

Filling

200g	GF mince meat *

Mincemeat tip: Mix in a couple of tablespoons of ground almonds and/or some sherry or brandy to the mincemeat prior to placing in the pastry for extra special pies!

PREPARATIONS

1. Blend the dry ingredients together in a bowl.

2. Rub in the butter/spread until it resembles fine breadcrumbs, then stir in the sugar.

3. Add the cold water and bring together into a ball. Add more water if needed until the pastry is formed.

4. Knead lightly, then roll out carefully in all directions with a gf floured rolling pin and surface until about 3mm thick. Do not attempt to move or turn the pastry. Cut 12 bases and 12 star shapes for the top. You will need to reroll a couple of times to cut all the bases and stars.

5. Using a palette knife, lift and place the bases onto a greased mince pie tray and press gently into position. Put a heaped teaspoon of mincemeat in each one and place a star shape on each pie.

6. Bake for 20-25 minutes at 175°C (fan oven), and the pastry should be golden.

7. Remove from the oven and leave to cool for 5 minutes in the tray, then transfer to a cooling rack using a blunt knife.

8. Dust with icing sugar and serve OR allow to cool completely and freeze.

The thud of the hut door as it finally closes for the night.
Curling up in the top bunk under layers of crocheted blankets with the
sweet smell of pipe tobacco and the sound of grown-up laughter as I
drift off to sleep.

ACKNOWLEDGEMENTS

There are many lovely people who are part of this Coeliac adventure with me.

Thanks first go to David, who, on my diagnosis, emptied our kitchen of gluten and joined me in the whole GF experience! Twenty years on, he is still by and on my side.

To my children, now adults, who caringly included my needs so young and continue to do so.

For dear Sirkka-Liisa who simply said, 'You must come, and we will bake'. Our time spent together reminiscing and baking was just joyous. I will forever be grateful for all your love and support.

My mother and father, who lovingly brought me up, honouring both their cultures and handing on their old family recipes, which have been part of my life and through this book, will continue to be so.

My two sisters who always enjoy the old and the new cake offerings at our meet-ups. Through shared times, we continue to enjoy being together, whatever life throws at us.

To Paul at SALTS Diner, who believed in me enough to buy over 2000 of my cakes. At a time when it was not so common, he felt it important to stock a selection of GF cakes.

For my friends Jane, Jackie and Ann who have always understood the emotions and feelings behind being a Coeliac and continue to support me as life inevitably changes and provides us with new challenges as we get older.

And lastly, I'd like to thank you for your interest in my journey, and I hope it will help you along the way with your journey.

Johanna, Summer 2024

Printed in Great Britain
by Amazon

59762876R00097